This Candlewick Book Belongs To:

_____

What NOT to bring when you watch birds!

uncomfy shoes

What? boop boop

noisy things
(You need to listen!)

Wait... you want me to stand around and look at birds like... OUTSIDE? SERIOUSLY?

All right, there's a bird. Watch it. OK, can we go now?

this friend

What Do You Need to Watch Birds?

Hardly anything! Mostly you need:

eyes →
ears →

(or some combination of the two)

Oh, and your brain, of course!

And then there's stuff for drawing and taking notes...

pens and pencils

Don't forget a pencil sharpener!

FIELD GUIDE

something to keep it all together

A sketchbook— big enough for lots of notes, small enough to be easy to carry

Spiral-bound with a hard back works best.

your trusty field guide

and here are some other useful things!

Sunscreen

bug spray

Something waterproof to sit on... an old jacket is fine.

a hat

granola

your snack of choice

Wait a sec.... Aren't you going to tell them they need cool binoculars like mine?

Well...no! You don't need super-expensive binoculars. There are many good ones that are quite affordable, and I hope you can get a pair someday. But you don't need a pair to start!

Oh, phooey! I keep losing them—these birds won't stay still! They keep flitting around!

Binoculars take time to learn how use. In the meant there is so much learn without ther Practice seein the whole bird... its shape, size, t way it moves... before you worr about all the litt details.

Bird-Watching Do's . . . and Don't's!

Do only go to places you know are safe.

Do be respectful of birds, nature, and other bird-watchers.

Do sit quietly and move slowly.

Do try to be inconspicuous, and try to blend in with the scenery.

Do try to be friendly to other bird-watchers! They are generally a pretty nice bunch of people.

Do be patient! You might not identify every bird that comes along, and that's all right. Every time you go out, you'll learn a little more.

Do give birds their space!

Do check for ticks when you get home!

For Dave and James

First revised paperback edition 2019

Library of Congress Catalog Card Number 2012942416
ISBN 978-0-7636-4561-8 (original hardcover edition)
ISBN 978-0-7636-9300-8 (revised paperback edition)

20 21 22 23 24 LEO 10 9 8 7 6 5 4 3

Printed in Heshan, Guangdong, China

This book was typeset in Sabon.
The illustrations were done in ink and watercolor.

Candlewick Press
99 Dover Street
Somerville, Massachusetts 02144

visit us at www.candlewick.com

And now, a very special thank-you to our good friend Jim Barton!

Yes! Thank you, Jim! Because of you I have these totally proper wing bars!

Check 'em out!

During the preparation and proofing of this book, I benefited from the technical assistance of Jim Barton from Cambridge, Massachusetts, a veteran birder with forty-five years of experience. For many years, Jim has led field trips and taught bird identification for the Boston office of the Massachusetts Audubon Society, the Friends of Mount Auburn Cemetery, the Cambridge public schools, and the Brookline Bird Club.

Hey, how come you drew him all nice and I look like this? Look at this bill.

It's just not acceptable!

Aw—c'mon, guys! Sometimes you have to make sacrifices for humor!

I only have THREE toes!

TALK to her, Mr. Barton

Contents

BONUS: More Bird-Watching Activities and Tips!

I'm gonna go check out the rest of the book and see if she got everything else right.

Oh, no! All our secrets!

Here are all the reasons it's better to watch us birds than other critters!
1. More exciting than slugs!
2. More varieties than squirrels!
3. Less dangerous than grizzly bears!
You're not going to let him eat that right here on the opening page, are you? He'll gross everyone out!
Just warning you... roadkill aheac Hope you're no squeamish!
What's THAT supposed to mean? Eating dead stuff is natural and beautiful.
C'mon, you guys, why can't you be nice and cute and quiet like these little guys on the other page?

This is a book about one of my favorite hobbies: bird-watching (and bird drawing, too!).

But I should warn you right up front, I'm not a professor of ornithology (which is the fancy name for "study of birds") or anything like that. I'm not an expert bird-watcher — not a single pair of my binoculars even works properly! I just really love birds.

I wasn't always a bird-watcher, but several years ago, I thought it would be nice to keep a nature sketchbook. When I sat outside to draw trees and rocks and flowers, I couldn't help but begin to notice lots of birds, some I knew and some I didn't, flitting around the edges of my drawings.

Had they been there all along, and I just hadn't been paying attention?

I couldn't stop watching them, and before I knew it, I was hooked.

Oh, I know what you're thinking....

I saw some bird-watchers in the park once. Whatever!

PRETEND THIS IS YOU.

Why would I want to watch birds, anyway? Looks kinda boring.

Bird-watching is NOT boring! Is a hawk swooping down to gobble a mouse boring? Of course not. And how about crows getting into your neighbor's garbage? Also not boring . . . Those birds are really smart! (OK, you should probably go shoo them away. . . .)

Birds are, by far, the easiest-to-see of all wild creatures. No matter how small your corner of the world, there will be some birds in it. You might be amazed at just how thrilling it can be to see new birds, find out about them, and learn their names!

And while you're out here, why don't you try drawing birds, too? C'mon, it's fun!

WHAT IS THE POINT OF ALL THIS?

The point is . . . spending time outside observing life and drawing in a sketchbook can help you to see the world in a whole new way. You've always known that the birds and the trees and the insects and the rocks were there . . . but when you take the time to sit and patiently draw them, you do more than see them: you experience them. You feel yourself more connected to the natural world, more at home in it.

Some people think that nature is something experienced by *other* people — people who live out in the country. But no matter where you live, you are a part of the natural world, just as the birds and other creatures are. Your thoughts, feelings, and observations about nature are just as valid as anyone else's. You're the only one who can keep track of your specific experiences, so keep your sketchbook with you, write things down, and draw pictures. It's important.

A Great Place to Start

You don't have to go anywhere fancy to watch birds! No matter where you live, chances are, there's a lot more going on in your yard or on your street than you suspect.

What kinds of places are within walking distance of your house? Is there an old barn near you? It could be home to swifts, swallows, or maybe even a Barn Owl! If you're lucky enough to live near a marshy pond, keep your eyes open for Pied-billed Grebes, Great Blue Herons, and Red-winged Blackbirds. Anywhere that's a little different may have different birds!

Wing tip

Look in places where you usually don't, like low, under bushes, or high up, in the top branches of trees. Look *when* you usually don't, too . . . like early in the morning or just before dusk. You may find you don't know your own yard or your own street nearly as well as you thought you did!

Yeah, well, that's great for people with yards! What about people like me? How can I be a bird-watcher in the city, when all I can see out of my window is that one crummy tree there with little brown birds in it?
Well, let's start with those little brown birds. Do you know all there is to know about them? Are they finches or sparrows? Do you know which are the boys and which are the girls?
Do you know what they eat, where they live, if they stay all winter? Have you seen any babies? What sorts of noises do they make?
Are those pesky birds pooping on my windowsill again?

You may not have a yard, but you do have the sky. Look up! Many hawks, falcons, and even owls make their homes in the city.

City birds are tough and adaptive—meaning they make do with what they find. Little birds like pigeons and sparrows eat what they find on the streets; birds of prey hunt *them* from high perches atop buildings.

City birds aren't picky about where they live, either! Look closely and you may see a Mourning Dove nesting in an old pot on a terrace, an American Kestrel raising its babies behind a gargoyle, or sparrows and starlings taking up residence in any empty spot they can find.

A Northern Mockingbird may be found singing in any high spot.

No one likes pigeons, but they are clever and resourceful!

Starlings

Here is a hawk zeroing in on her prey.

What is that racket?

You might see the House Finch. The male has a rosy red breast.

The House Sparrow is probably the #1 most common city bird!

LAW OFFICE 871

So there you are, out behind your house or somewhere on your street, sitting in a quiet spot with your sketchbook, patiently waiting for the birds to show themselves. But once they turn up, what should you do?

The most important thing is to keep quiet and pay attention. Once you've had a chance to look closely, use sketches and little notes to yourself to keep a record in your notebook of the birds you see.

park down the street next to school

eye is yellow

body is nice reddish brown

June 29 late afternoon

long tail

pointy bill

streaky spots

ate a bug

hopping aroun

Try to sketch while keeping your eyes on the bird as much as you can. This takes practice, but it's so worth doing. Don't worry about how "good" your picture is—the act of drawing is valuable no matter what the result looks like, because when we draw, we look extra, extra hard, and that helps us focus our attention. There's so much to pay attention to—shape, color, sound, and more! So let's take each aspect one at a time.

9

A Rainbow of Color

We crows and ravens will be good and stay out of the color chart, as we are totally sharp super-black...

Lots of birds, like us guys here, have nice red decorations!

Redhead Woodpecker

Red-winged Blackbird

Rose-breasted Grosbeak

Common Redpoll

Hooded Oriole

Orange means one thing... orioles! Did you know we're related to blackbirds?

Baltimore Oriole

Unlike some other "black" birds I know, who insist on wearing ridiculous disco outfits!

Yellow-headed Blackbird

Eastern Meadowlark

Western Meadowlark

Blue-winged Warbler

Prothonotary Warbler

Yellow Warbler

He's just jealous!

Black-billed Magpie

Green Jay

Lewis's Woodpecker

Steller's Jay

Great-tailed Grackle

Tree Swallow

European Starling

I'm covered with colorful speckles... like stars!

Blue Jay

Pinyon Jay

We grackles, magpies, and starlings look black from a distance, but our feathers are iridescent, showing shiny metallic colors up close.

'Cuz I'm the STARling. Get it? Clever, huh?

Purple Martin

Look Closely

Color can be a great way to identify birds. Even if you don't get a good look at a bird, a quick flash of red might be enough to tell you that you may have spotted a cardinal. Just remember that colors can look different in different light, especially in the late afternoon or evening, or if the bird is in deep shade. Also, note that sometimes male and female birds don't look alike — males are often brighter.

Don't forget black and white!

Black-footed Albatross

Audubon's Shearwater

Magnificent Frigatebird

Northern Gannet

Brandt's Cormorant

California Gull

Common Tern

Black Skimmer

White-tailed Tropicbird

Atlantic Puffin

Common Eider

Western Grebe

Surf Scoter

Common Murre

Black Scoter

Common Loon

Bufflehead

I drew all these birds together to make a nice picture, but many of these birds, like the Puffins and the Tropicbird, don't really live even remotely near each other.

Be a birdbrain

It isn't a coincidence that so many seabirds are gray or blackish on top and lighter below. This coloration works to their advantage, helping to hide them from the fish they're hunting and from other birds. (Many seabirds, like the Magnificent Frigatebird, are notorious for sneaking up and trying to steal one another's food. In fact, Frigatebirds are named after the type of ships pirates used!)

And then there's BROWN, too!

Birds will show you a whole world of brown! Look closely and you will soon be a connoisseur of this color. Study our bird color wheel and see how brown can be almost black . . . dark like tree bark or mottled like leaves . . . lovely russety-red or almost pink . . . golden like autumn grass . . . dusty and gray and plain as a mouse . . . or pale as sand.

> Oh, look at all the poor dears, the color of dirt! So sad for them!

Be a birdbrain

Why do you think so many birds are so many different kinds of brown, with all manners of streaks and spots? Can you think of any advantages for brown birds?

> No one here but us moldy leaves!

13

Shapes Are Clues

Many birds have characteristic silhouettes, whether perching on a wire, sitting on the water, or flying. How many of these shapes have you seen?

Yellow Warbler

House Wren

Song Sparrow

Barn Swallow

Tree Swallow

Eastern Kingbird

Eastern Phoebe

Mourning Dove

Rock Dove (Pigeon)

Belted Kingfisher

Red-tailed Hawk

The Great Blue Heron flies in an unhurried, gentlemanly manner, neck neatly folded.

Kingfisher hovering

Downy Woodpecker

Great Blue Heron

Ibises fly with necks out!

Double-crested Cormorant

Cormorants and Anhingas both stand with their wings spread to dry.

Ospreys hover to hunt. You might see one carrying a fish!

Hairy Woodpecker

White Ibis

Black-crowned Night Heron (neck folded)

Cormorants swim low in the water.

Mute Swan (More famous swan shape)

The Anhinga swims even lower; it looks like a snake sticking up.

Tundra Swan

The Turkey Vulture is famous for flying in a V shape, called a dihedral.

Here is a Herring Gull, a typical seagull.

American Crow

People say "as the crow flies" because crows fly fast and straight.

The Common Raven also flies as if she has important business to get to.

Terns are a bit pointier.

Common Tern

The Mourning Dove, like all pigeons and doves, is also a strong, fast flier.

Nighthawks and Chimney Swifts fly erratically, which means this way and that.

Flickers fly in a great swoopy up-and-down way! This is called undulating flight.

A flock of Brown Pelicans flies as though they are being pulled along on a string. They are lovely to watch.

Hummingbirds zip around like tiny manic helicopters!

Look Closely

Try to capture the general shape of a bird in your sketchbook, and take note of how it flies: Is its flight fast and powerful or weak and clumsy? Is the bird agile? Does it dart about gracefully? Does it dive? Think about the shape of its body, and especially the shape of its wings. Does the shape of its wings have anything to do with how it flies?

15

Take note of the general shape of the bird you're looking at. Is it . . .

round and
plump?

short and
sturdy?

thin and
sneaky?

short-legged and
long necked?

Then consider all those other interestingly shaped important bird parts, like bills. Is the bird's bill . . .

a straight,
strong chisel?

thin, delicate
tweezers?

a tearing
hook?

a scoopy
shovel?

What about feet? What kind of feet does the bird you're looking at have? Are they . . .

big, scary
clawed feet?

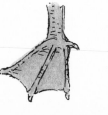

flipper feet?

climbing feet?

little gripping,
perching feet?

strong walkin'
feet?

16

Some birds sport fanciful hairdos and cool little hats (field guides call 'em crests).

The Pileated
Woodpecker wears
a jaunty cap!

The Wood Duck
is looking fine!

The Northern
Cardinal wears a
little bishop's miter.

We're like the Incredible Hulks of the avian world!

Yeah! You see the crests up, you gonna get messed up!

Some crests are small and secret, like
those of the Orange-crowned Warbler
and Ruby-crowned Kinglet, and only shown
when the bird is feeling aggressive.

Many of these crests are quite eye-catching!

It's called a
PLUME. I assure you,
it's QUITE NOBLE.

Some quails wear
a neat little
deely-bopper kind
of hat.

The Greater
Roadrunner's crest
adds to his rakish
good looks.

The Great Horned
Owl has "horns" that
are quite great.

Why is he
looking at me
like that?

The Horned Lark
has horns that
are quite wee.

Anything else interesting? Tails, perhaps? Take note!

Um, it's
not my tail.

I just have
extra-long wing
feathers.

Cranes wear
bustles, like
old-timey ladies.

Well,
dearie, it
LOOKS like
a tail!

Hey,
lady, watch
out for your
bustle!

Scissor-tailed
Flycatcher

These are some
good tails, but mine is,
you know... GREAT.

Just
sayin'.

Great-tailed
Grackle

What Are They Up To?

Learning about birds goes far beyond noticing what they look like. When we watch birds closely—when we see how they move, eat, communicate, build their nests—this is called observing their behavior, and it's what scientists do!

You have probably done a bit of this already. Imagine it is very early morning, and there are birds in your yard. They are hopping a bit, maybe running around, stopping, cocking their heads, and pulling up worms. Do you know who they are?

You may not be able to see them very clearly, but the way they're acting can give you some clues. Birds are predictable—you won't catch an eagle hopping around on your lawn, pulling up worms! Those birds in your yard are exhibiting classic robin behavior.

I know who those guys are— I see them every day!

This is why you shouldn't feel bad if you're not able to get out and see many new birds. If you get to know your most familiar neighbors really, really well, then you will be all the more ready to notice something different should anyone new happen by. (This is one of the most important things I can tell you.)

When you're paying attention to a bird's behavior, one of the most obvious things you'll notice is who it spends its time with. The robin is a social bird—he likes to be with others of his same kind, which is called being gregarious. For social birds like this, there can be safety in numbers, as well as advantages in locating and foraging for food.

Chickadees are also social birds who enjoy the company of their close relatives. (These groups are called mixed flocks.)

Crows roost together by the hundreds.

Cliff Swallows build their own mud apartment houses!

But not all birds are like that! Some are much more territorial, preferring to be the only ones on the block.

You might think wrens are little and cute, but they're really tough guys.

Mockingbirds are pretty aggressive, too!

Hawks are mostly solitary, but some will occasionally hunt with their mates or in other small family groups.

Speaking of hawks, here is a behavior you might see sometime. It is called mobbing, and it's when little birds band together to drive a bigger bird—like a hawk—out of town!

Individually, we're just little, but TOGETHER we're a mighty force!

Move along, buddy! This is a nice neighborhood!

GIT! GIT!

All right, already! Sheesh!

Here are a few other behaviors you might be able to see....

Male pigeons strut about with their feathers fluffed out. This is called displaying, and it's how they attract a mate.

Oh, my!

I bet HE could find some crumbs!

Oh...my poor wing! Woe is me!

I sure hope there are no cats around!

Birds in springtime gather grasses, twigs, and moss for nest building.

A Killdeer will pretend to have a broken wing to lure a predator away from her nest.

Wing tip

Bird behavior is a fascinating subject to read about! Every species has its own way of doing things — gathering food, attracting a mate, building a nest (or not, like those vultures on the right). Learn about their lives, and your understanding of birds will be all the richer.

Cuddle up next to that nice hard rock, dear!

Note the Fine Details

So I'm trying to identify these birds here...

There's that kid with the bowl cut again.

Yeah, I'd know him anywhere.

...but they all look the same to me! They're all little and brown. Though wait... if I look really closely, I can see one of them has a big spot on his tummy! Is that important?

I don't need a lot of silly doodads to feel pretty...

...but I do like to wear a tie on occasion!

As we saw on the rainbow page, very few birds are one solid color . . . yes, except for you, Mr. Crow, and Mr. Raven, and Mr. Purple Martin! Pretty much everyone else has varying shades of one color, or several colors, or a pattern of some sort. Even our plainest birds usually have a few markings . . . a little something special about their appearance so that they can recognize one another as members of their species. These are called field marks, and you can think of them as decorations, if you'd like!

Hey... Remember me and my fabulous hairdo?

Wood Duck

I'd sure HOPE I was the only one in the family to have a mustache!

Northern Flicker

Oops, just a bit of mustard.

The Sandwich Tern has a yellow spot on the end of her bill.

It's the layered look without the bulk!

The Dickcissel wears a tidy li'l dickie.

The Yellow-rumped Warbler has a bright yell___ ___t on his rump___ ___ble.

I BEG your pardon. Do I draw attention to YOUR rump?

REALLY now.

Foot note

Many field marks, like the Flicker's mustache, are worn by the male birds only. Out of the marks shown here, only those of the Sandwich Tern and the Yellow-rumped Warbler are worn by both sexes.

Though some field marks, like the Wood Duck's, are quite easy to see, you might have to look a little harder for the subtler ones. The more you practice, the more you will begin to see the differences among all those little brown birds.

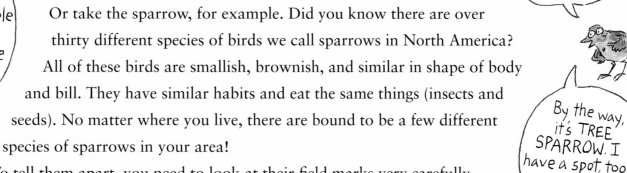

Or take the sparrow, for example. Did you know there are over thirty different species of birds we call sparrows in North America? All of these birds are smallish, brownish, and similar in shape of body and bill. They have similar habits and eat the same things (insects and seeds). No matter where you live, there are bound to be a few different species of sparrows in your area!

To tell them apart, you need to look at their field marks very carefully.

MODERN SPARROW
Hey, did I hear someone say they can't tell us apart? Maybe our fashion show will help!
How can people think we look alike? Really, now!
Yes! Imagine mistaking your big ol' football helmet for my sleek li'l Italian-style racing cap! Funny!
FOOTBALL HELMET?
And over here we have Chipping Sparrow in a clever red cap and very distinct white eyebrows!
American Tree Sparrow also sports a red cap and notched tail, and adds a stylish stick pin!
Starting us off today is Song Sparrow, working a rather severe look with the bold chest spot and streaking she is famous for...
Good thing you wore the bib. The bugs they're serving are pretty messy.
Oh, yeah, I always wear it to these things.
I could totally rock that look!
I just don't think I could pull that off!
But on her, it works!

Feathers 'n' Such

As we saw in the previous section, you can tell birds apart by their little details. But here's where things can get a bit complicated: a bird doesn't always look the same from one year to the next, or from one season to the next.

Think about people . . . and all the changes they go through as they grow up. Most people wear different clothes, depending on what life stage they're in. (Unless they're my friend Carl.)

Hey.

Birds change outfits, too! Only with them, it's feathers. This is called plumage.

Once they grow up, many birds keep the same look for the rest of their lives.

The male is often brighter than the female. Sometimes a lot brighter . . .

and sometimes just a little bit.

In a few pairs, the male and female don't appear to be the same species!

And in others, the sexes look exactly the same.

Many other birds wear a flashier look in spring and summer, called breeding plumage.

. . . or just a few fanciful plumes, like these Double-crested Cormorants have.

This brighter look helps to attract a mate, and it can be a whole new colorful outfit, like the male Scarlet Tanager's . . .

Listen Closely

When you go out to look at birds, make sure you listen to them, too! Their singing can be lovely to hear, of course, but they sing to communicate with one another, not just to sound pretty. Think of all the ways birds use sound.

HEY! THIS IS MY BRANCH!

And so's this one, so KEEP OFF!

I'm a catch! I know a lot of songs, and I sing 'em all pretty nice!

Oh, ladies... listen to me!

Here's a little ditty I learned from dear ol' dad....

They sing to establish their territory and to advertise themselves to a potential mate.

Hi! I'm over here!

I'm over here!

Birds call to keep in touch with one another, and to warn one another of danger. Maybe they're talking to you, too!

Hand over the sandwich, ma'am.

CAT!

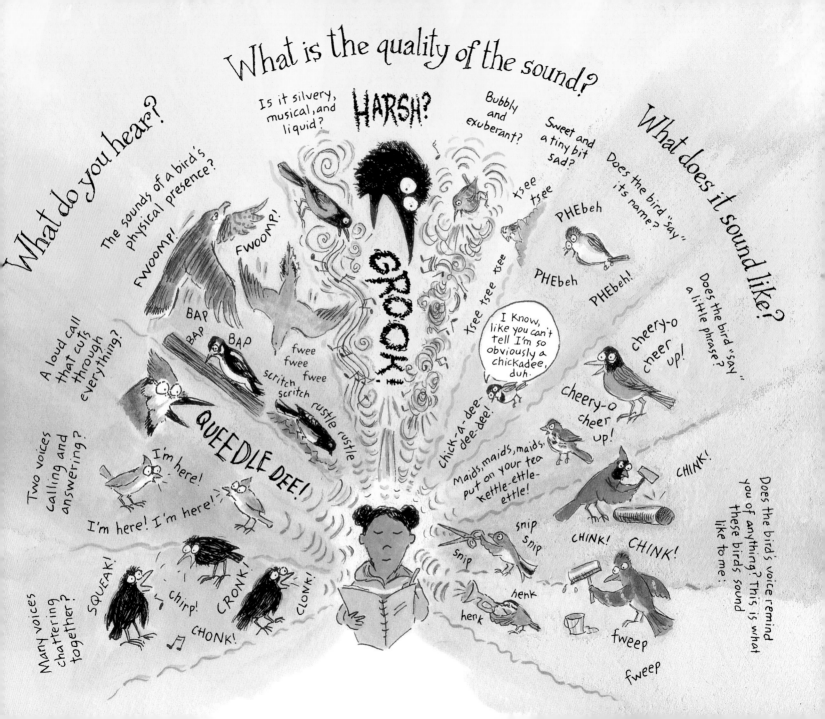

Time for a Field Guide!

Now that you're becoming more aware of all the birds in your area, and you're noticing all their various shapes and colors and habits and songs . . . is it occurring to you that there are a lot more birds around than you thought? Maybe you've seen some new ones and you'd like to learn their names . . . but how can you do that? You could ask a local bird-watcher, if you know one. Or you could crack open a field guide!

A Field Guide to the Birds of Whidbey Island

Field guides are great to have. They'll tell you everything you need to know about a bird and help you make sense of all your observations. Your local library probably has a few to look at. Some field guides might make you feel overwhelmed at first; you might want to start with a beginner's guide or one with birds more specific to your area. Most are arranged by families, which will help you to narrow down what bird it is that you are trying to identify.

The Beginner's Book of Backyard Birds

Every Single Bird Who Lives On or Has Ever Visited This Continent

Here's a whole bunch of birds that look kind of like the one I saw... It was probably a sparrow.

Or was it a warbler? Whoa...There's TONS of them!

Hey..."Worm-eating Warbler!" That's funny.

Most field guides will give both common and scientific names.

A good guide will show if there are various plumages, and tell you if the male and female don't look alike.

There will be a physical description, with field marks to look for and facts about voice, behaviors, diet, and nesting habits . . . all that good stuff!

Chipping Sparrow
Spizella passerina

Red cap
White wing bars
Notched tail

Juvenile
First winter
Winter non-breeding

Known for his red cap, notched tail, and call of rapidly trilled "chip" notes. Little flocks of them are commonly found in yards, shrubbery, fields, and open woodlands. Diet consists of insects in summer and grass and weeds in winter. Nest is a finely woven cup of grasses and hair, found 25 feet up in a tree.

Most will have range maps showing where the bird is found and where it goes if it migrates.

So . . . who was that cute little guy I saw on the lawn?

Hmm . . . my bird kind of looks like a Seaside Sparrow. Wait a minute, I live in Iowa, so that seems unlikely . . . .

Brewer's Sparrow? Nah . . . says here they live in mountain meadows, so that's also unlikely. Ditto for Sage Sparrow, I suppose . . .

Keep trying, Kid!

Wing tip

If you buy a field guide, take it with you when you go out to look at birds! But try not to waste time looking up birds in a book when the actual birds are right in front of you — you don't want anything to distract you from watching the real birds carefully, and there'll be plenty of time to look them up in your field guide after they've flown away!

The Power of Observation

Let's take a look now at two very distinct birds. We'll compare their various attributes and see all the ways they are different from each other—and what those differences mean to the birds.

A bird looks the way it does for a reason. You can often figure out what—or who!—a bird eats and how it spends its time by paying attention to what it looks like.

One of the best places to look for birds whose features are adapted to their environment is by the water. It's clear that these birds are fish eaters!

Pelicans scoop fish out of the water with their pouches!

I stab at thee!

Cormorants can swallow fish and eels thicker than their own throats!

The Black Skimmer skims fish right from the water's surface.

Herons wade into the water with their long legs, then wait patiently and strike with their daggerlike bills!

On the other hand, a cardinal's no fisherman . . . you can tell just by looking at him.

What's THAT?

First of all, fish would find that bright red color alarming!

Help!

The cardinal has pointy little perching feet, no good for swimming!

Oh yes... very funny, ha ha. Who wants to eat a dumb squid anyway?

This is NOT working!

And even if he caught a fish, he could never hold on to it with that stumpy, chunky bill of his!

Just as we saw with the various seabirds, birds generally eat what they are best adapted to eat. Each bird has developed specialized "tools"—bills and feet—that help it get its favorite foods.

Some thrashers' bills are like pickaxes for digging in hard soil for bugs.

Purple Gallinules have super-long toes for walking on floating vegetation.

Owls and hawks kill with their powerful feet and sharp talons.

Much better than squid!

Cardinals' thick, strong bills are perfect for cracking nuts and seeds.

Don't forget my chiselly bill and my long, sticky bug-grabbing tongue!

Those dumb bugs don't stand a chance!

Wrens have thin, curved bills for extracting insects from crevices.

Woodpeckers' feet are specially adapted for climbing and clinging to vertical surfaces. Even their tails help them balance as they climb.

All parrots are quite adept at using their feet like hands!

Who are the most highly specialized birds of all? They may well be vultures and condors! Although many people find them . . . uh . . . a little icky and creepy, due to their somewhat unpleasant habits, they have some extremely efficient adaptations for eating carrion (that means dead stuff).

These birds help to keep the earth clean by eating things no other bird will eat . . . and that's not icky or creepy at all! In fact, maybe there's something beautiful about it.

"Creepy"?

Strong hooked bill for tearing flesh

Big strong wings for endless soaring in search of food

The bird's small head can be thrust deep into carcasses; its naked skin is easier to keep clean than feathers.

Yep... that's been there a week now! You know I like a bit of carrion now and again, but I have my limits! It's all yours, buddy!

Mmph— yep, that was a stinky one, all right! Smelled it a mile away.

Their stomachs are able to digest REALLY putrid meat filled with noxious microbes.

Turkey vultures can locate food by smell!

Be a birdbrain

When you look at a bird, keep in mind all the things we have studied: size, shape, color, pattern, way of moving. Can you see how it's equipped to make its living? Can you make predictions about what it eats and how it gets that meal?

Where Birds Are At: Habitat

If you visit different parts of your town, you may notice that the birds in your yard are different from the ones down the street, or in the supermarket parking lot, or at the soccer field, or wherever. That's because every bird has a certain environment that suits it best for how it lives and what it eats. This environment is called a habitat. Consider the Roadrunner:

She can build her nest in a cactus!

Her body is extremely efficient, so she doesn't need much water.

Mmmm! I do love a juicy smashed-up snake!

Her drab, mottled plumage helps her to blend in with her dry, dusty surroundings.

Her long legs and big strong feet are ideal for running quickly over hard, open terrain.

As you can see, the desert is a good place for a Roadrunner! Here are some other birds who live in very specific places. . . .

Kingfishers nest in long tunnels they dig into riverbanks. They also need the river for fishing.

The river can't be TOO fast, or TOO shallow, or TOO deep.

It has to be perfect. Not that I'm picky.

The American Dipper needs a fast-moving, somewhat shallow stream for foraging.

Here I am, the noble Spruce Grouse, in a spruce grove, eatin' some spruce needles.

Yep yep yep.

The Spruce Grouse . . . enough said.

Birds are thought to be "successful" if they can adapt to living in all sorts of places and can eat what they find in those places.

Other birds' diets are much more tied to their habitat, and so they are much less flexible and, unfortunately, more likely to be endangered.

Both the Greater and Lesser Prairie Chickens need open prairies for food and nesting.

The Snail Kite's curved bill is perfect for eating apple snails, which are found in the marshlands of Florida.

37

Home in the Range

Although you can see quite a variety of birds by seeking out different habitats near where you live, you generally need to be within a bird's range—the geographical area in which it is typically found—to see it.

Because I live in New England...

I must face facts and accept that I will not see a flamingo flying over my house, or a California Quail trotting through my yard, or a penguin swimming at the beach.

It's sad, but...

I will console myself with the thought that I could see an Atlantic Puffin, if I wanted!

I mean, I would have to drive a long way and then take a ferry ride... but still, I could!

Remember Ms. Roadrunner? Her range is strictly southern . . . from California to Arkansas and Louisiana, and down into Mexico. She thrives in dry, open habitats like desert and grasslands. The Southwest is her range because that's where she finds her required food and shelter.

Well, I should <u>hope</u> they would remember me! I was just on the last page. Good grief.

A bird who is less dependent on a specific habitat may well have a larger range, like our fine, charming friend, the ubiquitous European Starling, who is found throughout the U.S. and Canada, visible just about anywhere there are people.

Ubiquitous? Is that like debonair? I *am* European....

Check out my year-round range! Pretty big, huh? Yep, anywhere you people are, I'm probably going to be there, too!

I like living in your cities, your towns... and I LOVE your farms! I like all your stuff! I LOVE you guys!

Probably just about everyone in North America has seen a starling . . . but what about a few of these other very common birds, who also have very large ranges?

Uh, so... here we are again, Mr. Owl!

Do NOT trust him.

Huh... says here the Great Horned Owl and the Horned Lark are both widespread and common...

It's awesome for you to know our ranges...

...and jeepers, Belted Kingfishers, too! Why haven't I seen any of these guys?

but you still have to seek us out in our proper habitats!

Wanna come see my river?

Wing tip

If you have a family vacation coming up, you might get a chance to see birds that don't live in your area! (Remember to always bring your sketchbook and drawing materials on trips!) Zoos, aquariums, and natural history museums can also be great places to learn about birds you might not otherwise see.

North America is a very large continent!

And it's very geographically diverse. As many as 800 species of birds may call it home at any given time (though some are just passin' through), and some of them have very specific habitats and therefore very specific ranges. This map shows a few!

Do birds read our silly maps? No! Their ranges change all the time, sometimes expanding, like that of the Cardinal, and sometimes shrinking, like that of the Snail Kite, which is now endangered in the U.S.

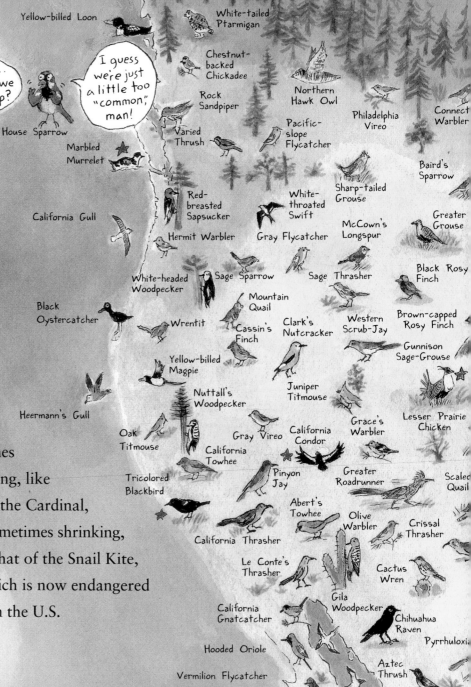

To You It's Vacation; to Us It's Migration!

Have you ever noticed that the birds you see in summer may not be the same ones you see in winter? Many birds migrate, traveling a lot (or just a little) to find better weather, more food, or their traditional breeding grounds. If you live in the northern part of the United States (like me), you've probably noticed there are fewer birds around in winter. But because most birds fly south, there are a few kinds of birds I actually see more of in the winter, like Dark-eyed Juncos. They migrate from Canada to Massachusetts . . . because even though it's wintry and cold where I am, it's still warmer than it is in Canada!

> So nice and cool up here in the summer! A bit too cold for me in the winter, though... maybe I'll go to Annette's house!

> I hate to travel! It's just right here.

> I hope I remember the way to Texas!

Most field guides will have maps with a key showing different information like this:

- ■ Summer or breeding range
- ☐ Winter range
- ▢ Migration range
- ▨ Year-round range
- ⊙ "Rare" or "accidental" sightings

> Hoo boy! That was some storm! I wonder where the heck I am?

> OK... I'm gonna get something to eat, rest up, get my bearings...

> I wonder if you can get good squid around here.

Rare sightings can happen when a bird gets blown off course. Maybe an albatross will pop up in your yard someday! You never know. . . .

Some birds make migratory trips of almost unbelievable lengths. Don't be too quick to dismiss that little brown sparrow—she could be resting up from an amazing journey!

Arctic Terns spend the summer up here...

then fly all the way down to Antarctica...

where they spend the winter (the Antarctic summer)...

then fly all the way back again!

The Arctic Terns are a very dramatic example—they may fly 31,000 miles every year!

Other birds, like these puffins, migrate just a bit.

Be a birdbrain

Think about the birds you see around you in all the seasons. Who's there in spring, making nests? Are you part of their breeding range? Maybe you see some birds for only a few days in the fall because you're a stop on their migration route. And what about winter—who stays, and who goes? If it's warm where you are, do you get an influx of winter residents?

45

When scientists classify life-forms, they group them together in a series of categories. These groups start off very large and general, then are organized into smaller and smaller subgroups as the life-forms inside them become more and more alike by scientific standards.

Scientists estimate there may be as many as 20 million different life-forms on Earth (most are molds, bacteria, and insects . . . but still!), and they've only officially classified about a million and a half of them! With such an amazing variety of life, you can see how important it is for scientists to have a way to keep track of everything!

Even though he's very closely related to the other birds in his genus, Lincoln's Sparrow and Swamp Sparrow, the Song Sparrow is still very much his own species. He looks like a Song Sparrow, sings Song Sparrow songs, has a lady Song Sparrow for his mate, and raises baby Song Sparrows. That's what it means to be *Melospiza melodia*, to use his scientific name.

– AHEM! – Uh, one might also say "Linnaean name," because I, Carolus Linnaeus, had the totally cool idea to name all living things this way.

Y'see, back in the 1700s, scientists were naming critters all willy-nilly, and it was a big mess. So I said, "Dudes, this is nuts. From now on, let's have names be two words denoting genus and species, and it will be totally official and totally awesome!"

Thanks, Mr. L.! Great idea! Not that we birds need those big fancy names or anything....We know they're just for you humans!

Though I have to say, I really do love my name, Melodia...melody...like in a song! Song Sparrow! Get it? It totally suits me, right?

It's fun when birds' names tell little stories about them! Here are a few more. . . .

The Wood Duck's Latin name, Aix sponsa, means "Duck who is betrothed."

The Northern Mockingbird's Latin name, Mimus polyglottus, means "many-tongued mimic."

The Dark-eyed Junco's Latin name, Junco hyemalis, means "Junco of the winter."

And here are a few easy scientific names for you to learn!

Well, here we are, at the end of everything I have room to tell you! I hope this book has helped to start you on your way to watching and drawing birds . . . and I hope that experiencing the natural world and keeping a sketchbook will bring you great joy for all the years of your life, too!

You can be any kind of bird-watcher you want to be—you might spend your life searching for rare birds, or you might just like to check out your local sparrows every now and then. It's up to you!

50

Always remember that you are part of this world . . .
so grab your faithful sketchbook, get out there,
and take a look around!

Bibliography

Wait a minute—I'm supposed to eat worms?

This book grew from my own observations and experiences sketching birds, but I read many books along the way to help me with my drawing and writing.

How to Know the Birds: An Introduction to Bird Recognition by Roger Tory Peterson. Boston: Houghton Mifflin, 1962.
  Everyone interested in bird-watching should own this book.
There isn't a friendlier, more charming introduction anywhere.
The writing is an absolute delight, and the pictures are so helpful.
Don't ask me why I thought there was anything else to add!

Should've added some emus.

The Sibley Guide to Bird Life and Behavior, illustrated by David Sibley. New York: Knopf, 2001.
  This book is stuffed to the brim with facts and beautiful pictures. It was indispensable to me.

Birdsong: A Natural History by Don Stap. New York: Scribner, 2005.
  This wonderful book explains how and why birds sing.

Naming Nature: The Clash Between Instinct and Science by Carol Kaesuk Yoon. New York: Norton, 2009.
  I loved learning about the way all life-forms are related, and why it's important.

The Birds Around Us, edited by Alice Mace. San Francisco: Ortho Books, 1986.
  The chapter "Changes Through Time" by Kimball L. Garrett taught me about the whole flamingo-duck-heron business.

Mr. Sibley's drawings are much nicer than the ones in this book—

he actually draws the right number of toes!

And I couldn't have drawn all my pictures, both the funny and serious ones, without consulting field guides! The ones I used the most were:

Field Guide to the Birds of North America by the National Geographic Society. Washington, D.C.: National Geographic, 1999.
  This book has the loveliest pictures.

The Sibley Guide to Birds by David Allen Sibley. New York: Knopf, 2000.
  Again, I would be lost without Sibley! I went through this book so much, the cover fell off!

Peterson First Guide to Birds of North America by Roger Tory Peterson. Boston: Houghton Mifflin, 1986.
  This is the field guide that truly got me started.

Birds: A Guide to Familiar American Birds by Herbert S. Zim and Ira N. Gabrielson, New York: Golden, 1987.
  You can learn a lot from these little Golden Guides!

I was the first bird she looked up!

That's why she has a special place in her heart for us starlings!

The website I consulted most often was the Cornell Lab of Ornithology's, at www.allaboutbirds.org. I used this when I wanted up-to-the-minute information about names, habitats, endangered status, that sort of thing. You can listen to birdsongs and watch videos, too!

Index

Hey, if you're ever in Phoenix, look me up!

I'll look you up right now... in the index!

I always thought it was "morning dove".

Now I feel sad!

I see we sparrows are very well represented...

'cause we RULE! We're way better than those silly warblers!

Only TWO pages for my magnificence? That does not seem right.

Shoot!

EIGHT pages, buddy! Just sayin'!

Hrumph!

More Bird-Watching Activities and Tips

If you love birds and want to see more of them, the next step is to find ways to get them to come to you. You can do this by making your home a welcoming place—like a real habitat. The following activities will help you discover ways to feed, provide water for, and shelter birds.

You will also find tips to help you draw birds and make maps of your backyard or any places you like to watch birds. Try the scavenger hunt to make your bird-watching even more fun!

The More You Help Them, the More You'll See Them!

Think of what a hard world it is out there for birds! Birds are often threatened by habitat loss. This means they have fewer places to establish territories, make homes, raise their families, and find foods that they like.

Feed and shelter birds, and you will doubtless be helping them more than you know. You may be helping an exhausted mother feed her babies, or another bird eat when natural foods are not available, or another fatten up before a long journey south.

When we help birds, it's good for us, too!

Helping birds helps the environment and makes our homes more natural, beautiful places.

And you'll be able to track birds coming and going any time of day, any time of year from the comfort of your home!

Feel free to do nice things for us!

We totally love it!

Last one in is a rotten egg!

I love what they've done to the place! Even put in a pool!

uh...

I'm SO glad we found this rest stop!

What's the best way to get us to come to your yard?

FEED US!

Feeding birds is a wonderful thing to do! There is a great variety of feeders one can buy; some are very simple, and some are very expensive and complicated. Just remember: different birds eat different foods and will use different kinds of feeders. And should you feel bad if you start feeding birds and then stop?

We're cool! And flexible! We'll just go nosh at your neighbors'!

NO!

← These little cage feeders hold squares of suet (beef fat) that are especially enjoyed by woodpeckers.

These thin cylinder feeders are often filled with black niger seed and are very popular with small birds like goldfinches.

Hopper-style feeders keep the seed dry inside plates of Plexiglass.

These feeders hold nectar (sugar water) and are just for hummingbirds.

The ground is a good place for small seed like millet, as well as bread crumbs and cracked corn, for ground-feeding birds like doves, sparrows, and quail.

A platform feeder has a flat surface with a raised edge for keeping the food from falling off. This is a good place for sunflower seeds, which are enjoyed by most larger birds.

Some of us birds actually prefer to eat on the ground!

Yeah, too crazy up there—way too much competition!

Filling feeders with seed you buy from a store can be expensive, and keeping them filled can be a lot of work! Don't feel bad if you can't keep feeders (I don't have any because we get bears!); there are still some other ways to feed birds, if you want!

Feeding us doesn't have to be complicated! Why not just share some of that food you may have lying around the house?

Fruit chunks

An orange half stuck to a branch

Peanuts in the shell (not salted) threaded onto string

Popcorn

Chunks of fruit like melon, apples, and bananas

Grapes

Any kind of berry

Be careful: fruit will spoil quickly in hot weather!

Baked potatoes in skins

Smashed-up dog biscuits

Cooked rice

A hollowed-out orange filled with grape jelly

Food can be placed on a platform feeder or just scattered on the ground.

Half a coconut (You could hang one on a tree, too!)

Bread crumbs, bits of stale baked goods like banana bread or donuts

Mmm... peanut-butter-and-jelly sandwich crusts! Can't believe you don't eat these!

You share your food, we delight you with our adorable antics!

Sounds fair to me!

How about trying to make one of these simple feeders yourself?

A clean mayonnaise jar hung from a tree by a twisted clothes hanger

A milk carton or a plastic milk jug with windows cut out, filled with seed

A pinecone covered in peanut butter (You could even roll it in seed after)

You can hang suet in a mesh bag that fruit comes in!

SUET

is a very important food for birds, especially in colder weather, because it gives them energy to keep warm. You can buy it in premade squares at a grocery store, then make your own suet cakes by melting it in a pan on the stove, mixing it with seeds or dried fruit, and letting it harden in an old muffin tin or other container. Some people mix suet with peanut butter and cornmeal, then stuff that mixture into holes in trees for woodpeckers, nuthatches, and chickadees to find.

Remember: suet is for cooler weather only! If it's too warm, it can melt and go rancid.

Ooh, and it can make a terrible mess when it gets all over our feathers and stuff!

Yum! This is a very happy surprise!

Feeders and Birdbaths: Your Responsibilities

Keep them clean! Remove damp seed, because it can get moldy and spread disease. Change birdbath water often. Both feeders and baths may need to be scrubbed occasionally.

Place them where birds can take shelter quickly — but not where predators might hide!

HELLO! Some privacy, please!

Hmm... that PBJ made me kind of thirsty! A little bit of **WATER** would be nice!

Birds of all kinds love a birdbath! Water is necessary not just for drinking but for bathing, too. Birds need to keep their feathers clean!

The birdbaths you see sold in stores are great, but if you can't have one of those, almost any shallow dish, like the dish that goes underneath a flowerpot, for example, will do! (And many birds prefer to bathe on the ground.)

A trash-can lid (metal or plastic) makes a great birdbath!

A few rocks inside for birds to stand on are much appreciated.

Make sure the water is no more than two inches deep!

You can put some rocks on the side to make it stable.

Can You Grow Some Flowers?

A flower garden will not only make your home more beautiful; it will also make it a more welcoming habitat for birds and provide them with important natural food sources. Gardening is a wonderful lifelong hobby that can go hand in hand with bird-watching! It does not take a lot of space to grow some flowers. Here are a few that are very easy to grow.

You know what we woodpeckers love? DEAD trees! They're full of bugs! If you have a dead tree, can you leave it for us?

Gardening Tips

Let part of your yard go wild! Is there a part of your yard where a few wildflowers can grow free? Yes, most adults think of them as weeds, but they are a super-important part of the food chain, and many are pretty in their own way! (Of course, the grown-ups of the house would have to be on board here.)

Most flowers need lots of sun, but some prefer shade. It will say on the plant tag or seed packet.

Be patient! It can take months for plants to grow and bloom, and sometimes years for a garden to be how you'd like it.

Start small! If a garden is too much work or if you don't have a yard, you can always grow flowers in pots—on a deck or terrace or a fire escape. Even in a window box!

Trumpet vine

Our Favorites!

Queen Anne's lace

Thistles

Dandelions

Asters

Red clover

Did you know monarch butterflies lay their eggs ONLY on milkweed plants?

Milkweed

Jewelweed

If you have any kind of milkweed plants (and there are many) PLEASE leave them be!

Bugle-weed

We wouldn't say no to some dead leaves and a bunch of old branches!

Leave us a little empty dirt, too! We love a dust bath!

How About Providing a Nest Box?

A challenge facing many birds is the scarcity of good nesting sites. More human houses usually means fewer trees and fewer places for birds to raise their families. So hanging a nest box or two can really help! Not all birds will use a nest box, but here are a few different kinds and the birds that will use them.

FINALLY a house in a good neighborhood can afford!

It's perfect!

A wren or phoebe may make a home in a dried gourd.

I'm not sure I will enjoy living next to owls.

A long wooden nest box that mimics a hollow tree limb may be a good home for an owl!

Birds that nest in tree cavities, like chickadees, wrens, nuthatches, and woodpeckers, will use enclosed boxes like these.

Birds that don't like an enclosed space, like robins or swifts, may appreciate the shelter of a simple shelf.

Drat! I forgot our apartment number again!

Oh, I met them; they're very nice.

Purple Martins prefer to live together in bird apartment buildings.

Houses like these have really helped to bring bluebirds back from a very serious decline.

Maybe You Could Build One Yourself!

Me, I'm not so good at making stuff out of wood! But maybe you are!

I say call the building inspector!

Making a nest box is a great first woodworking project! There are many simple kits available from woodworking and hardware stores, or you can download plans from the Cornell Lab of Ornithology (http://nestwatch.org/learn/all-about-birdhouses/). Cornell has different plans for the specific kind of bird you would like to attract. (Did you know, for example, that the size of the entrance hole will help determine the type of bird that will use your house?)

Here are some other tips! The nest box does not have to be fancy. It should not be painted or stained. There should only be one entrance hole (but ventilation holes near the top and drainage holes on the bottom are a good idea). Do not put in any nesting materials—birds will think someone else already lives there!

If your box does get used, make sure you clean it out at the end of the season!

No back door because we do NOT care for any unexpected guests!

Like those awful SNAKES!

Hanging your nest box is the tricky part! Some birds are SUPER picky about where their nest is located!

PICKY? Moi? Oh, not at all!

I mean, SURE, we like things just so—who doesn't?

But we're not picky! Of course, a little sun is nice, but not TOO much—we don't want to be too hot! A little shade would help, but not too shady! And please put us at least five feet off the ground.... That's not asking too much! And it doesn't have to be EXACTLY five feet, just, well, four is definitely too low, and, once you hit seven it's a whole different thing...

Some Thoughts About Bird Drawing

Grrr! Drawing birds is too hard! I'm giving up!

No! No! Don't give up!

I know it's hard! Trust me, I've drawn some pretty weird birds in my time!

Let me give you a wee bit of advice...

Because I don't want this to be you →

When we draw a bird or any other living creature, we begin by finding the general shape of its body.

Ducks really are such a nice shape to draw. ↓

Lots of drawing books say "start with an oval," and lots of birds are kind of oval-shaped!

← Many little birds don't have much of a neck!

Getting the shape right is half the battle! →

Laughing Gulls are a kind of triangular shape, like a paper hat on the water.

Birds that are black are great to draw!

You won't be distracted by details if you draw crows, starlings, and grackles! They're all about shape and posture!

C'mon... this tail is GOOD, but not yet GREAT!

I do like to give them → mad faces!

Practice drawing the birds you see every day. But try to see them with fresh eyes!

Are the wings held up or down?

Is the tail short or long?

Is it a pointy bill?

How do the legs fit into the body?

Big feet!

For example, you might think you know robins, but do you? Look at a robin like you've never seen one before!

Oh my goodness, it's Uncle Joe!

How About Drawing a Map of Your Yard?

As you're learning to draw birds, you can also use your sketchbook to keep a record of the birds you see. Do this, and not only will your knowledge grow, but you will also begin to more deeply understand birds' habitats and the cycles of nature throughout the year.

If you don't have a yard, think about the place you see birds most — on your street or at the closest habitat you can visit, like your school or local park.

This is my yard here.

Pileated Woodpecker

WE HAVE BEARS!

SPOOKY OWL NOISES
Are they Barred Owls or Great Horned Owls? Not sure! I'll have to listen to the Cornell Lab of Ornithology site to find out!

Blue Jays!

FWEEP!

My favorite bird, the Great Crested Flycatcher, has been seen here.

I see warblers here in the fall but not during the summer. Are they migrating?

very tall white pine

I find owl pellets here sometimes.

Mroww!

Catbirds love it here! And I love catbirds!

crab apple tree

tangly weedy bushes

In the time we've lived here, many, many more robins stay for the whole winter. What does this mean?

Baby Grumpy

Hopalong Grumpy, the wicked groundhog who eats my petunias, lives here. →

Saw a Ruffed Grouse...once!

In spring, I always hear this pair of orioles before I see them!

There was a family of Red-tailed Hawks way up in this tree once! The babies cried morning till night!

HUGE OAK TREE

very tall pine tree

Sometimes a hawk will patiently wait way up in a tree for a chipmunk to pop out of this little hole.

(You don't want to know what happens, trust me.)

Chickadees, titmice, and nuthatches all live in this tree! There was even a pair of Wood Ducks once!

Wild turkeys eat the acorns in the fall.

Baby turkeys— SO CUTE!

My butterfly bush attracts hummingbirds, hawk moths, and butterflies.

Juniper

My hummingbird garden

Lots of wrens here! They eat the bugs between the cracks in the wall.

Mourning Doves and House Sparrows eat bugs on my patio.

I make note of the birds who stay all year as well as ones I see only in the winter or summer, along with ones I have seen only once or twice—those I check in my field guide. For example, I learned that the Pine Grosbeaks I saw in 2001 (I wrote it down!) are a rare occurrence! My field guide says I am living on the very edge of their winter range. And the White-throated Sparrows I see in winter: Did they migrate from the north, or do I just notice them more?

Bird-Watching Scavenger Hunt!

Have You Ever Seen?

☐ A bird that is red
☐ A bird that is blue
☐ A bird that is yellow
☐ A bird that is yellow only on its tummy
☐ A bird that is somewhat greenish
☐ A pigeon that is all white (or almost all white, among all the other pigeons)
☐ A bird that is black and white
☐ A whole tree full of crows
☐ Baby Canada Geese (my husband thinks they look like fuzzy little tennis balls)
☐ Seagulls in a parking lot, all standing around thinking they're tough guys (so not!)
☐ A baby robin in the grass
☐ A vulture flying in big circles
☐ A bird with hardly any head feathers
☐ A crazy bird you have NO idea what it is
☐ A bush or tree all filled with the same kind of bird
☐ A bird sitting so quietly you almost didn't see it
☐ A bird living in the letters of a store sign
☐ A bird with red eyes

Don't say crows, that would totally be cheating.

OK, now I know I don't have to tell you this, because obviously you are a very smart kid, but do NOT check off any of these boxes if this is not your own personal book! You can make a copy of this page and do it, OK?

I know... nag, nag, nag! I can't help it!

How many of these have you seen...

☐ A teeny-tiny bird?
☐ A bird with a spot?
☐ A bird with many spots?
☐ One that is a bit more streaky?
☐ A bird with a tail that sticks up?
☐ A bird with a very long neck?
☐ Or a bird that looks like it's wearing pants?
☐ Or with very big feet?
☐ A bird with a bill like this?
☐ Or one like this?
☐ A bird with an extremely teeny bill?
☐ A very long and pointy bill?
☐ A long pointy tail?
☐ A bird with a very long neck and very long legs?
☐ How about a stripey tail?
☐ A bird with a stripe through its eye?
☐ A bird with a crest?
☐ A bird that you first thought was a mouse?

SUPER STORE

How Many of These Behaviors Have You Seen?

- ☐ A bird with a stick in its bill
- ☐ A bird of prey carrying something in its feet
- ☐ A parent bird feeding babies
- ☐ A seagull stealing a French fry
- ☐ Crows "mobbing" a hawk
- ☐ A robin pulling up a worm
- ☐ (check here if you watched for a while and it was a lot of worms)
- ☐ A bird taking a dust bath
- ☐ Starlings flying in a big shape
- ☐ A bird hunting a bug
- ☐ A duck with just its behind sticking up out of the water
- ☐ A vulture eating roadkill
- ☐ (check here if it was something gross)
- ☐ Little birds stealing crumbs at an outdoor restaurant
- ☐ A pigeon strutting around thinking it's all that
- ☐ Crows poking around in the trash
- ☐ A hummingbird drinking from a flower
- ☐ (check here if it was the cutest thing ever!)
- ☐ A woodpecker pecking a house
- ☐ A seagull dropping something in the road on purpose
- ☐ Canada Geese flying in a big V
- ☐ A bird taking a bath in a puddle
- ☐ A bird catching a bug in the air
- ☐ A crow proudly carrying off a donut (it doesn't have to be a whole donut)

Did you know robins listen for worms?

This is called a "murmuration"

I wish it were a whole donut!

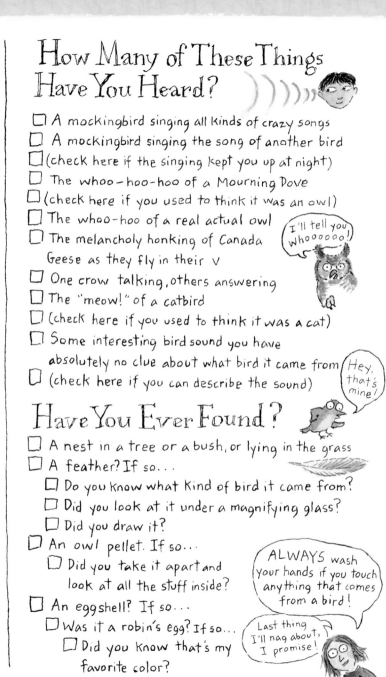

How Many of These Things Have You Heard?

- ☐ A mockingbird singing all kinds of crazy songs
- ☐ A mockingbird singing the song of another bird
- ☐ (check here if the singing kept you up at night)
- ☐ The whoo-hoo-hoo of a Mourning Dove
- ☐ (check here if you used to think it was an owl)
- ☐ The whoo-hoo of a real actual owl
- ☐ The melancholy honking of Canada Geese as they fly in their V
- ☐ One crow talking, others answering
- ☐ The "meow!" of a catbird
- ☐ (check here if you used to think it was a cat)
- ☐ Some interesting bird sound you have absolutely no clue about what bird it came from
- ☐ (check here if you can describe the sound)

I'll tell you whoooooo!

Hey, that's mine!

Have You Ever Found?

- ☐ A nest in a tree or a bush, or lying in the grass
- ☐ A feather? If so...
  - ☐ Do you know what kind of bird it came from?
  - ☐ Did you look at it under a magnifying glass?
  - ☐ Did you draw it?
- ☐ An owl pellet. If so...
  - ☐ Did you take it apart and look at all the stuff inside?
- ☐ An eggshell? If so...
  - ☐ Was it a robin's egg? If so...
    - ☐ Did you know that's my favorite color?

ALWAYS wash your hands if you touch anything that comes from a bird!

Last thing I'll nag about, I promise!

Some Bird-Watching Tips!

Check out your library or community center for bird talks and programs. Sometimes you may be able to see real raptors!

Go on a guided bird walk!
Is there a conservation area or an Audubon center near you? See if they have a website. There may be organized walks with bird experts from time to time.

Keep your eyes peeled on long car trips. You will almost always see hawks or vultures in the sky. (I like to count how many Red-tailed Hawks I see in trees per mile.)

On long drives, rest stops can be great places to see birds! When you are in a new place, always remember to look in "regular" places, like playgrounds and supermarket parking lots. Always check out the birds on telephone lines!

And even more bird-watching tips

Practice listening to birds... and following their voices until you see them. This takes practice, but it is a great skill to have, getting your ears and eyes to work together!

Listen to all the sounds a bird makes: little feet climbing a tree trunk, wing beats, and quiet footsteps in leaves. A chipmunk rustling sounds much different than a bird walking slowly and deliberately through leaves!

You're getting warmer!

No!   Yes!

When you are outside, try to keep low and not stand out too much.

Avoid looking directly into the sun! It's bad for your eyes, and seeing details will be nearly impossible. Always check out sources of water: even drainage ditches and especially large puddles!

Hey! That looks like a SWALLOW tail!

Not being able to identify a species is NOT a failure! You are learning even if you guess. You are learning even if you just carefully watch birds go about their everyday business. Don't worry too much about identification. Just enjoy being in nature!

Some more stuff to do...

indoors...

Go online to the Cornell Lab of Ornithology site (www.allaboutbirds.com) and listen to the sounds of any bird you can imagine! (And speaking of Cornell, the website has all sorts of interesting programs for kids to take part in, like Project Feederwatch. Check it out!)

Ha... Penguins make the craziest noises!

urk!

How about Screech Owls?

Do they really screech?

Do you have a pen pal or relative who lives far away? They may have a favorite bird — ask them sometime!

We have quail where we live. They are super cute!

I'll draw you one!

(You could also draw a picture of your favorite bird and send it to your friend or relative in a letter. Maybe they'll send you a picture back!)

Do you have a vacation coming up? Research the birds you might see so you'll be ready to see some new birds when you get there!

I'll be waiting for you!

Someday I'm gonna send a picture to "Birds and Blooms"!

Find a bird-watching book or magazine at your library. These resources may have great advice for feeding and watching birds!

and out!

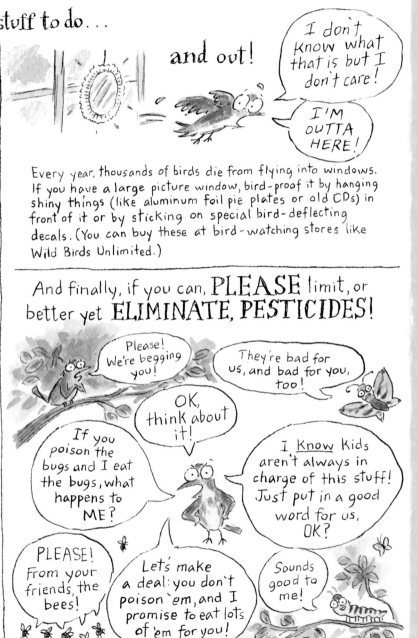

I don't know what that is but I don't care!

I'M OUTTA HERE!

Every year, thousands of birds die from flying into windows. If you have a large picture window, bird-proof it by hanging shiny things (like aluminum foil pie plates or old CDs) in front of it or by sticking on special bird-deflecting decals. (You can buy these at bird-watching stores like Wild Birds Unlimited.)

And finally, if you can, PLEASE limit, or better yet ELIMINATE, PESTICIDES!

Please! We're begging you!

They're bad for us, and bad for you, too!

OK, think about it!

If you poison the bugs and I eat the bugs, what happens to ME?

I know kids aren't always in charge of this stuff! Just put in a good word for us, OK?

PLEASE! From your friends, the bees!

Let's make a deal: you don't poison 'em, and I promise to eat lots of 'em for you!

Sounds good to me!

Some last tips for you...

Remember, birds can be anywhere! Every bird will have its own habitat, its own special place to be.

Some birds will be high up in trees, some low.

Some will be in high grass or bushes

And some will be on the ground.

(And if you don't see any birds, practice drawing rocks, trees, bushes, squirrels...)

Always look if you see wiggly leafy branches!

Some birds will only be found in treetops!

Baseball and soccer fields are great places to look for birds.

Cemeteries, too!

One of the best things about bird-watching is that it's a hobby that you can have for your whole life. And if you keep sketchbooks, you'll have a record of your lifelong pursuit, and that will be an amazing thing to have! In six months, a year... twenty years... you'll be able to look back and remember...

Oh, yeah... this was back in Ohio...

...the first time I saw a Rose-breasted Grosbeak! I'll never forget that.

Wow, my drawing has really improved since then!

So many birds out there, and so few people see them! Be one of the people who see them. Good luck, keep looking, and keep drawing!

A HUGE THANK YOU!

to Andrea Tompa and Pam Consolazio (the editor and designer of this book) for their unfailing enthusiasm and support. This would not be the book it is without their hard work and endless enthusiasm!

They're the best!

Yay!

Thank you so much, Andrea, for having faith in this project!

So... um... could this be a book?

Hmm.. yes!

And thanks to Pam, for not minding all the teensy scraps of paper!

Oops

Found some more.

No problem!

Thank you also to my great friends and to my very wonderful family. I am so lucky to have you all. And a special thank-you to my friend Catherine M. Connors, PhD (University of Washington, Department of Classics), for her help with the Latin, and for sending me books. And, finally...

Well, I'm glad somebody cares what my Latin name means!

Which is "Bluish Diver," by the way!

Thanks, Bob!